The Odyssey:
A Reader's Guide to the Homer Epic

ROBERT CRAYOLA

Copyright © 2014 Robert Crayola

All rights reserved.

ISBN: 150241290X
ISBN-13: 978-1502412904

CONTENTS

INTRODUCTION	1
THE ELEMENTS OF LITERATURE	4
CHARACTERS	8
CHAPTER SUMMARIES & COMMENTARY	12
CRITICAL QUESTIONS & ESSAY TOPICS	38
CONCLUSION	41

INTRODUCTION

The Odyssey is a fundamental text in the history of Western Literature. It lays the ground for the entire genre of the "adventure" story, and it is an exciting, humorous, and fascinating story to this day. In this guide we will look at *The Odyssey* from a variety of angles, learning about the culture that produced this story, the history taking place at the time. Furthermore, we'll look at the elements of literature that make up the whole, so when you read the text you get a bigger picture and find deeper meaning in the narrative. My purpose is to help you understand the confusing parts and make the story as enjoyable and memorable as possible.

You can use this guide before or after reading the book. I will reveal major plot details, however, so if you don't want spoilers, read the book first.

AUTHOR & CONTEXT: According to classical tradition, a blind singer named Homer was the author of both *The Iliad* and *The Odyssey*. The Greek historian Herodotus claimed that Homer lived around 850 BC. Since that time there has been skepticism about Homer's age and origins, his authorship, and even his existence. The original versions of the epics attributed to Homer were probably conceived in an oral (spoken) tradition, with many changes and additional material added as the story was told and retold. While there might have been one person to conceive of the overall structure, the entire epic is probably best viewed as the work of a generation of bards (spoken-word performers). Written in an earlier form of Greek known as Homeric Greek, *The Odyssey* is believed to have been set in its current form by the Greek tyrant Peisistratos in the sixth century BC.

As for the story itself, ancient Greeks thought the Trojan War occurred in the 12th or 13th century BC. The site of Troy is now believed to be at Hisarlik, in Turkey, thanks to excavations by Heinrich Schliemann. Whether there actually was a Trojan War, however, is less certain.

THE TROJAN WAR: The Trojan War of myth sets the stage for *The Odyssey* and is also one of the most famous stories in Greek mythology.

The Trojan prince Paris was selected by the gods to settle a debate over who was the fairest goddess: Hera, Athena, or Aphrodite. The goddesses each tried to bribe the man, and Aphrodite's offer to give him Helen of Sparta, the most beautiful woman in the world, made Paris choose Aphrodite.

The Trojan prince Paris took Helen of Troy from the Greek king Menalaus, launching the ten-year war between the Greeks (Achaeans) and Trojans. The war's end was chronicled in the other work attributed to Homer, *The Iliad*. The most famous incident from the war was the sacking of Troy by hiding warriors in a large wooden horse ("the Trojan horse"). Among the warriors in the horse was Odysseus. Following the war, *The Odyssey* chronicles the voyage Odysseus to his homeland of Ithaca, an isle off of Greece.

THE ELEMENTS OF LITERATURE

STRUCTURE: *The Odyssey* is divided into 24 sections. The structure is very innovative for the era, employing flashbacks and multiple points of view. The story begins on Ithaca and follows Odysseus's son Telemachus as he searches for word of his father. The perspective then shifts to Odysseus until he meet the Phaecians, and then he recounts his travels after the Trojan War. The book's final sections detail his homecoming to Ithaca.

The book is written in as an epic poem in *dactylic hexameter*.

SETTING: The book takes place in and around the Mediterranean. Troy (also referred to as Ilion or Ilium) is in modern day Turkey. The islands that Odysseus visits are throughout the Mediterranean. Ithaca is off the west coast of Greece.

The time is approximately 1200 BC.

NARRATOR & P.O.V.: The book is written in the third-person, but much of the book has Odysseus recounting his own story, and these sections use the first-person perspective.

TENSE: The book is written in the past tense.

TONE: Tone is how a book "feels." This is an epic and has an epic feel. Everything is larger than life, important, and set against the background of life's drama, tragedy, and glory.

PLOT: The plot is the book's story. Here is a quick snapshot of the plot. We'll take a deeper look in the chapter summaries.

The Odyssey is the story of Odysseus's return to his home of Ithaca after the ten-year Trojan War. His son Telemachus and wife Penelope fear he is dead. To learn what has become of Odysseus, Telemachus travels to speak with Odysseus's companions from the war.

Odysseus has been stuck on the island of the nymph Calypso. He is finally allowed to leave, nearly dying on the ocean, until he arrives at the land of the Phaecians. They welcome him and he tells of the many misfortunes and challenges he and his crew faced after the war. All of these events were caused by his blinding of Polyphemous the Cyclops, son of Poseidon (god of the sea). The Phaecians agree to help Odysseus home, but pay for their aid with their lives.

Arriving home in Ithaca, Odysseus disguises himself as a beggar to learn who he can trust. His home is overrun by men who want to marry his wife. He holds a shooting contest that only he can win, and then he kills all the suitors. This causes great unrest among the families of the men Odysseus has killed, but Athena buts an end to any further violence.

That is an extremely shortened version of the story, but it gives you a general idea of where it is going. We'll look at a more detailed version of the plot soon.

PROTAGONIST: The protagonist is the main

character or characters that we most sympathize with. Odysseus is the main protagonist. His son Telemachus and wife Penelope are also protagonists.

ANTAGONIST: The antagonist opposes the protagonists. Odysseus faces many enemies in the book in the form of men, monsters, and gods (mainly Poseidon).

CONFLICT: Conflict is the struggle faced by the characters. Most of the book's struggle is derived from Odysseus's attempt to make it safely home to his family and restore order.

CLIMAX: The climax is the moment of greatest tension in the story. This point is reached when Odysseus has suffered endless abuse at the hands of the suitors and will take no more. He wins the shooting contest and reveals his identity, going on to kill all the suitors.

RESOLUTION: The resolution is how the story concludes after the climax has passed. Once the suitors are dead, Odysseus and those loyal to his household remove the suitors and clean the house. Odysseus travels to his father's home and is sought out by people seeking to avenge the suitors. The goddess Athena intervenes and stops any further bloodshed, and Odysseus rules as king of Ithaca once again.

THEMES: Themes are what the author chooses to illustrate through the narrative. Some of the themes in the novel include:

Perseverance toward goals – Odysseus faces innumerable obstacles on his way home but never loses sight of getting back to Ithaca.

Loyalty and connection – Penelope and Telemachus never forget Odysseus and refuse to move on with their lives until they know he is dead. Odysseus's friends and servants also display their loyalty. Those who fail to stay loyal generally suffer the consequences.

Honor – People treat guests with honor, show honor to the gods, and if they don't they are often punished.

The mind's ability to defeat brute force – Odysseus is known for strength and being a great warrior, but that isn't enough to defeat some challenges. He uses his mind to get past the Cyclops, the suitors, and other foes.

The journey and the return – Odysseus's departure and return to Ithaca, and how he changes in the process, can be viewed as a standard template for the hero's journey.

CHARACTERS

(Note: Spelling may vary depending on which translation you use.)

[handwritten: major characters]

ODYSSEUS – Odysseus is a great warrior who fought in the Trojan War. He is the main character in the book and he narrates several sections in the first-person. He will be away from home for twenty years before his return. Aside from his skill as a warrior, he is renowned for his cunning mind and way with words.

[handwritten: major]

TELEMACHUS – Telemachus is Odysseus's son, about twenty years old. He travels to visit Nestor and Menalaus and find word of his father.

[handwritten: major]

PENELOPE – Penelope is Odysseus's wife. Suitors are constantly at her house attempting to win her hand in marriage. She has refused them for years.

[handwritten: major]

ATHENA – Athena is the goddess of war. She is a great ally of Odysseus and often helps him. She pleads with the other gods to help him and she often takes the form of human characters to intervene directly.

ZEUS – Zeus is king of the gods and known as the god of the sky and thunder. He is known to help Odysseus when Athena requests it, but he is also loyal to his brother Poseidon.

major

POSEIDON – Poseidon is the god of the seas and brother to Zeus. He is also the father of Polyphemous the Cyclops. He hates Odysseus for injuring his son.

medium

NESTOR – Nestor is the king of Pylos and an old friend of Odysseus. Telemachus seeks him out for word of his father. Nestor is known for his wisdom.

medium

MENALAUS – Menalaus is king of Sparta and another friend of Odysseus from the Trojan War. Telemachus seeks him out early in the story. He is married to Helen (whose abduction by Prince Paris led to the Trojan War).

medium

HELEN – Helen is wife to Menalaus. She is famous for her beauty ("the face that launched a thousand ships"). She aids Telemachus in his search for Odysseus and interprets an omen.

medium

PISISTRATUS – Pisistratus is Nestor's son. He accompanies Telemachus on the land voyage to visit Menalaus.

AGAMEMNON – Agamemnon was Menalaus's brother and a great general and king. He commanded the Greek forces at Troy. After the war, he came home and was murdered by his wife Clytemnestra. Odysseus encounters his spirit in Hades.

NAUSICAA – Nausicaa is a young princess of the Phaecians. She discovers Odysseus when he washes ashore at Scheria and helps him.

ALCINOUS – Alcinous is king of the Phaecians. He is suspicious of Odysseus's identity. When Odysseus finally recounts his story, Alcinous agrees to help him sail home.

ARETE – Arete is the wise wife of Alcinous and queen of the Phaecians.

major

CALYPSO – Calypso is a nymph (or minor god) on the island of Ogygia. Odysseus arrives there and is her prisoner for seven years.

POLYPHEMOUS – Polyphemous is a Cyclops, a large one-eyed monster. He is the son of Poseidon. Odysseus blinds him and invokes the wrath of Polyphemous and Poseidon.

CIRCE – Circe is a witch. Odysseus's men arrive on her island and she turns them into pigs. Odysseus is able to overcome Circe by using a magical plant, and he becomes her lover until he can escape.

HELIOS – Helios is a titan, a god of the sun. Odysseus and his men arrive on his island and slaughter his sheep, incurring his wrath.

LAERTES – Laertes is Odysseus's father, greatly aged by his son's absence.

EUMAEUS – Eumaeus is the loyal swineherd of Odysseus. He will aid Odysseus in overcoming the suitors.

EURYCLEIA – Eurycleia is a loyal old maidservant of Odysseus. She recognizes him when she sees the scar on his leg.

ANTINOUS – Antinous is the leader of the suitors, known for his rudeness and cruelty. Odysseus kills him first among the suitors.

EURYMACHUS – Eurymachus is another key suitor.

AMPHINOMUS – Amphinomus is one of the more honorable suitors. Odysseus urges him to leave, but Athena keeps him there to be killed with the others.

MELANTHIUS – Melanthius is a rude goatherd who helps the suitors and abuses Odysseus (when the hero is disguised as a beggar). His treachery will lead to his killing with the suitors.

MELANTHO – Melantho is the sister of Melanthius. She is employed as a servant of Penelope.

She is rude and sleeps with Eurymachus.

PHILOETIUS – Philoetius is the main cowherd of Odysseus in Ithaca. He is loyal to Odysseus and helps him vanquish the suitors.

CHAPTER SUMMARIES & COMMENTARY

BOOK 1: In its original form, *The Odyssey* was not a printed book. It was spoken or sung by a poet who had memorized the story. This feat may seem fantastic to us, but to ancient people who were less likely to be literate, it seems to have been fairly common.

The speaker of *The Odyssey* begins his story by asking the Muse to sing through him, allowing him to tell his story in a skillful way. This story will concern Odysseus, a great warrior who fought in the Trojan War. Ten years have passed since that war ended and Odysseus still hasn't returned to his home in Ithaca (a Greek island). His wife Penelope and son Telemachus await him, but they fear he has died. The narrator tells us that Odysseus has not, however. He is being held by the nymph Calypso "who craved him for her own."

At Odysseus's home in Ithaca, Penelope is besieged by men who want to marry her. They eat her food and stay at her house. Odysseus's son Telemachus is disgusted by these men and wants his father to arrive home and exact vengeance. The gods see this situation and have pity (except for Poseidon, who holds a grudge against Odysseus). They send Athena (goddess of wisdom and war) to Telemachus and advise him.

Athena goes to Ithaca in the guise of a sailor, an old friend of Odysseus named Mentes. She advises Telemachus to order the men to leave the house of Odysseus. Furthermore, she suggests Telemachus go to seek word of his father in Pylos and Sparta. A wise man named Nestor and a king named Menalaus may have word of Odysseus. Once Mentes leaves, Telemachus suspects he was a god in a disguise.

After this, Telemachus finds Penelope complaining about the bard singing of the Trojan War. She is saddened by the war that took her husband away. Rather than support her, Telemachus says that she can go away if she doesn't want to hear it. When she is gone, Telemachus informs the suitors that he will disperse them the next day. The men are suspicious that something has occurred, that some news has come from the recent visitor (Mentes). Telemachus says that the man was only an old friend of Odysseus and that there is no news.

BOOK 2: Telemachus calls the assembly the next day. It has not been held since Odysseus left many years ago. A respected old man named Aegyptius praises Telemachus for trying to fill his father's shoes. Telemachus gives an account of the abuses the suitors have laid at his family's home. They eat the family's food and are not wanted. He asks the god Zeus for justice in removing the men.

Speaking for the suitors, Antinous rebukes Telemachus and his mother Penelope. She has refused to wed. He refers to a trick she pulled on them, promising to marry one of them when she finished weaving a fabric. But instead of completing the work, she undid it each night so it would never be completed. The suitors eventually discovered this. In Antinous's view, Penelope is seducing the suitors without marrying any of them. This might sound like a rapist's logic to our modern eye. Nevertheless, it seems normal for the period. Antinous asks that Penelope's father select a husband for her, since she seems unwilling to do so herself.

We can see from these passages that a woman's rights are limited in this era. Women are defined by their relationships to men, and without Odysseus present Penelope has only her son for protection. Telemachus is unable to remove the suitors physically, and has thus turned to the men of Ithaca to aid him in their removal.

There are predictions that Odysseus will return to Ithaca after nineteen years away. Omens in the form of eagles are interpreted as meaning Odysseus will soon come home. Some mock these predictions. The gods are on Telemachus's side, however. Although the meeting fails to remove the suitors from Penelope and Telemachus's home, they do help Telemachus to prepare for a journey – he will go to seek news of his father. The goddess Athena disguises herself as Mentor, an old friend of Odysseus, and advises Telemachus to prepare for a sea voyage. She finds men in town willing to help him.

The only person who knows Telemachus is leaving is Eurycleia, an old servant woman. She will only reveal to Penelope where her son has gone after a few weeks have passed. The suitors have mocked Telemachus for anything he might do to them, but with the gods on his side the young man is destined to wreak vengeance on the suitors.

BOOK 3: After a short sea voyage, Telemachus and

his crew arrive in Pylos. He is there to speak with Nestor, an old and respected friend of Odysseus. Telemachus is hesitant to speak to such an experienced man and feels inadequate. Athena urges him on, however, and gives him the courage to pursue his task.

Nestor greets the travelers. A feast is held to welcome them before any business can be discussed. Once they have been welcomed, Nestor inquires about the purpose of their visit. He is pleased to learn Telemachus is the son of Odysseus. He welcomes the young man as a near-equal to his great father. Nestor tells of the return of the warriors from the Trojan War. They each dispersed in different ships and that was the last he saw of Odysseus.

Nestor understands Telemachus's desperation in seeking his father. Even in Pylos he has heard of the suitors inhabiting Odysseus's home and seeking Penelope's hand in marriage. Through his kindness and ability to see Telemachus's perspective, we see that Nestor is a truly wise man. He mentions Odysseus's favoring by the goddess Athena, and he encourages Telemachus in his search. Nestor urges him to seek Menalaus, the last of the leaders to return home from the Trojan War.

As Telemachus speaks to Nestor, he is accompanied by Athena (in disguise). Demonstrating hospitality, Nestor insists that they sleep at his home, not on their ship. Athena agrees that Telemachus should stay in the older man's house. Athena suddenly turns into a bird and flies away. Nestor and Telemachus know that the man must have been a god. This spurs Nestor on to aid Telemachus further. With a god aiding Telemachus, Nestor knows that anything may be accomplished.

Nestor honors Telemachus that night with a ritual feast for him and his crew. The next day, Nestor's son

Pisistratus accompanies Telemachus on the journey to Sparta to speak with Menalaus.

BOOK 4: Pisistratus and Telemachus travel in horse-drawn carriage to Menalaus's house. King Menalaus is in the midst of a double wedding feast for his son and daughter. Eteoneus greets the young men at the gate and checks with Menalaus to see if they should be greeted now, or cared for by someone else until Menalaus is free. Menalaus calls Eteoneus an idiot for even asking this. In Menalaus we see the hallmarks of the noble and polite man. He goes out of his way to make guests comfortable and give them honor, even before he knows exactly who they are.

The men enter Menalaus's house and find it very luxuriant and lavishly decorated. Menalaus speaks of when he and the others left Troy, and his great love and respect for Odysseus, which causes Telemachus to cry for his absent father. This (along with the physical resemblance) tells Menalaus that Telemachus is the son of Odysseus. The older man praises Odysseus for his wisdom. He tells them stories of the Trojan War that sheds a positive light on Telemachus's father.

They sleep that night. The next day Telemachus asks Menalaus if he has heard any news of Odysseus. In answer, Menalaus explains how he and his crew were detained in Egypt after the Trojan War. To learn why the gods were holding them up there, Eidothea, daughter of Proteus, told them how to capture Proteus and interrogate him. Proteus is a minor god, sometimes referred to as "the old man of the sea." By capturing and interrogating Proteus, Menalaus may learn what he has done to displease the gods. Once they catch Proteus in a trap, they learn they have displeased Zeus and the other gods by failing to pay proper homage before embarking on their voyage. Menalaus also asks Proteus what happened to the other great men who fought in the Trojan War. From this he learns that Odysseus is the captive of the nymph Calypso, and that Odysseus has lost his crew and ship and has no way of going home. This is more than Telemachus has ever heard about his father, and it offers hope that Odysseus may still be alive.

Menalaus asks the men to stay and enjoy his hospitality. Telemachus politely refuses and says his crew awaits him. Menalaus insists that Telemachus at least take a parting gift.

Back in Ithaca, a man named Noemon goes to the house of Odysseus. It is his ship that has been lent to Telemachus. He inquires among Penelope's suitors (asking Antinous) when Telemachus will return. Since Telemachus left in secret, the news that Telemachus has gone away is a surprise to the suitors. They are angered that the young man is acting against their will. They immediately plot to kill Telemachus for his cunning.

Penelope learns of their plans to kill her son. She is naturally distressed, and asks the gods for help. They console her by sending her a dream of Iphthime, a mythical figure. The dream woman assures Penelope that her son will be protected, and that Athena is looking after him. This is some consolation for Penelope, but when she asks about her husband Odysseus the dream figure is unable to provide an answer.

BOOK 5: Athena pleas with the gods to aid Odysseus. He is still being held captive by the goddess Calypso. Zeus, king of the gods, relents and sends Hermes to inform Calypso of the decision.

Calypso wants to keep Odysseus with her. She questions Hermes and says that the male gods have more rights than the females. Nevertheless, she submits to the authority of Zeus. As with humanity, the male gods hold more power than the females.

As for Odysseus, he still longs for home. Calypso asks if he really wants to leave – after all, his wife will grow old and die, but Calypso will stay young forever. Odysseus diplomatically explains that although Calypso is beautiful, he must go home. She agrees to help him. Odysseus is suspicious, but Calypso provides wood and tools for him to make a boat.

Odysseus floats on the ocean for over two weeks. Calypso has told him which stars to follow to reach Scheria, the land of the Phaecians. Poseidon, god of the sea, realizes that Odysseus is attempting to reach land and decides to abuse him. He has long had a grudge against Odysseus and he was away when the gods reached their decision to free the warrior. Poseidon does his best to destroy Odysseus with mighty waves, and Odysseus might have perished if he hadn't had help from Athena and another goddess – Ino, who in the form of a nymph named Leukothea gives Odysseus a veil to protect him. He uses it, and though his hands are ripped on the rocks, he survives his sea voyage.

Odysseus arrives at Scheria and a river god allows him access. He makes his way to land and finds rest once more.

BOOK 6: Odysseus sleeps on land. That night on Scheria, in the palace of king Alcinous, the princess Nausicaa has a dream. Visited by Athena in the form of her friend, she is prompted to take her clothes down to the river and have them cleaned. She is young and being courted by men and wants to look her best.

The next day, Nausicaa asks her father to take the mule cart and complete her plan, to which he agrees.

While Nausicaa and her maidservants are washing the clothes, they come upon Odysseus. He is in awe of the naked women and thinks he is dreaming. They too find him strange and want to know who he is. He asks them to excuse him so he may clean himself up. When they return they find him a changed man. Nausicaa finds him handsome and hopes to marry a man like him someday. She will take Odysseus to her father to be received. Odysseus prays for mercy from her people.

BOOK 7: Rather than accompany Nausicaa to her father the king and arouse suspicion, Odysseus remains in the city. He finds a young girl (Athena in disguise once again) who directs him to the palace. The girl praises queen Arete's wisdom and urges Odysseus to seek the queen's aid first.

Odysseus finds the palace rich and full of beauty. A festival for Poseidon is being held. He approaches Arete and throws himself at her mercy. A mist dissipates around him and the king and queen wonder if Odysseus is mortal or a god. On seeing he is a noble and well-spoken man, she and her husband offer to help them however they can, providing a ship to let him return to his homeland. They do not know his identity, only that he seems to be an honorable man.

Queen Arete notices Odysseus is wearing cloth that she herself has made. When asked about his, he tells the complete story of his journey since he left the goddess Calypso, until he was found by their daughter Nausicaa. The king and queen criticize Nausicaa for not bringing Odysseus to them directly, but the warrior defends their daughter and says he did not want to cause them anger. They say that this would never be, and that he could marry their daughter if he wished.

Once again (as with Nestor and Menalaus) we see the

graciousness extended to honored guests. Although Alcinous and Arete barely know Odysseus, they are impressed by his story and can see his is no common man.

BOOK 8: The next day Alcinous calls an assembly so men may learn of the stranger who has come to the island, a man who seems to be favored by the gods. A crew of the best men is assembled to help Odysseus sail home, although at this point nobody knows his identity.

There is a celebration and a minstrel sings. This was a common occurrence. The man sings of Odysseus in the Trojan War, unaware that the subject of his song is right there. The story brings Odysseus to tears and he does his best to conceal it.

Sporting games take place to impress Odysseus. Alcinous's son Laodamas challenges Odysseus to join them. A warrior named Seareach (or Broadsea, depending on which translation you use) uses a mocking tone to get Odysseus to compete. To show them he is capable, Odysseus hurtles a discus (a flying disc) and it goes farther than any other discus. The men are suitably impressed and they proceed to watch the dancers for which the island is famed.

A minstrel sings again. This time he tells the story of the married gods Hephaestus and Aphrodite, and her affair with Ares, the god of war. The story shows the value placed on honor, and also seems to put the blame for the affair on Aphrodite, not Ares.

A sword is presented to Odysseus, along with other items for his journey home. He is bathed, reminding him of the luxurious lifestyle he knew with Calypso.

Later, when the minstrel sings again, Odysseus asks that he sing of the Trojan War. The story brings more tears to Odysscus's eyes and king Alcinous asks the minstrel to stop to avoid distressing their guest. He finally must ask Odysseus who he is, why he weeps, and where the men are taking him on their sea voyage.

BOOK 9: Since he is compelled to answer, recalling all the grief of his travels, Odysseus begins a detailed account of his adventures since the end of the Trojan War.

He and his crew had intended to sail home as directly as they could. They stopped at Ismarus and raided the Cicones for supplies until their attacks are repelled and they were driven away.

Next they stopped in the land of the Lotus-eaters. Some of Odysseus's crew tasted the Lotus flowers. The effect made them forget what they were doing, why they were there, and they had no concern for their welfare or the future. Odysseus forcibly brought the men back to the ship and cautioned the others against eating the Lotus. This land can be viewed symbolically as the loss of purpose and destination. Odysseus would not have his will diluted. He was determined to get home.

The next island they saw had many sheep. They stopped to get food and supplies. A cave was particularly full of sheep. The crew wanted to grab the sheep and leave, but curiosity is a weakness (and simultaneously a strength) with Odysseus, and he took the men into the cave to explore. The cave's inhabitant soon confronted them. It was a gigantic Cyclops named Polyphemous, one of many such creatures that live on the island. He is the son of Poseidon, and this will prove important soon.

Polyphemous trapped the men in the cave by sealing the entrance with a large rock only he was strong enough to lift. He then ate two of Odysseus's men and promised to eat them all eventually. Odysseus wanted to avenge the men, but he must wait until the giant unseals the cave entrance.

The next day when Polyphemous is away, Odysseus makes a sharp weapon from some wood he finds. Then he got Polyphemous drunk on their wine. The creature asked Odysseus's name and he told the creature he is called "Nobody." When Polyphemous is drunk, he stabbed the monster in his enormous eye. Polyphemous was in agony and called out to his fellow Cyclopes for help. They asked what was wrong and he said that "Nobody" was killing him. If it was not a mortal killing him, then it must be the gods' will, so the other Cyclopes did not come to his aid.

Now blind, Polyphemous stood at the cave entrance so the men still couldn't escape. To get out, they tied themselves underneath the bellies of his sheep. When he felt the sheep as they came out, Polyphemous had no reason to suspect the men were underneath.

When the men were back on their ship, Odysseus could not resist hurling taunts at Polyphemous, loudly proclaiming that Odysseus was the one who blinded him. Polyphemous cursed Odysseus and asked that his father Poseidon (god of the seas) also curse Odysseus.

We see in this chapter that Odysseus is very tricky and intelligent, but that he is also recklessly curious and prideful. These traits allow him to survive many dangerous situations, but they also create those hazards in the first place. Still, he is admirable for his willingness to risk everything for the sake of adventure.

BOOK 10: Odysseus and his crew next stopped at the isle of Aeolus, king of the wind. They stayed there a month. Aeolus gave Odysseus a bag of wind to aid his travel. When they left, Odysseus kept a close eye on the bag of wind, refusing to sleep so his crew wouldn't have a chance to meddle with it. But eventually he had to sleep and the crew did just as he expected, opening the bag (they think it contains precious treasure) and blowing them all back to the island of Aeolus. It was doubly unfortunate because they were nearly in sight of Ithaca when the men opened the bag. Odysseus asked the king for more help, but it's clear to Aeolus that Odysseus is despised by the gods and he refused any further assistance.

Odysseus and his crew left, and their next stop was the island of the Lestrygonians. These are giants, and they devoured some of Odysseus's men. Odysseus and his remaining crew barely escaped with their lives.

The isle of Circe, a witch (or minor goddess), is their next stop. She lives on Aeaea. Odysseus sent scouts to explore the island and she turned the men into pigs. Odysseus knew it was dangerous to pursue the men, but he felt it was his only option. He was intercepted by Hermes, who gave Odysseus "moly" (a sacred plant) to protect him from the witch. Following Hermes's instructions, Odysseus was able to subdue Circe and force her to turn his men back into humans. Part of the agreement included Odysseus taking Circe as a lover. Much like the lotus flower eaten on the earlier isle by his men, Odysseus entered a trance-like state with Circe. They remained on the island for many months as seasons changed.

Finally his men urged him onward to home, and Circe agreed. She cautioned him that the route will not be direct, that he will have to go to the underworld and speak with Tiresias. The crew is dismayed to hear this. A further omen presents itself as one of Odysseus's crew, Elpenor, is killed when falling from a roof. Through these hints the story takes on a darker tone and a sense of foreboding.

BOOK 11: Following Circe's instructions, Odysseus's ship sailed to a place in the ocean where the "Men of Winter" reside and poured libations (liquid offerings), then dug up the earth, giving them access to the underworld where the dead reside. The first region was Erebus, where the recently dead reside. Odysseus saw Elpenor, who they recently left behind on Circe's isle. Odysseus promised to return to Circe's isle and give him a proper burial.

Odysseus sought out the blind prophet Tiresias, as instructed by Circe. Tiresias explained that Odysseus's troubles stem from Polyphemous, the Cyclops. By receiving his curse, Odysseus has been hounded by his father, the ocean god Poseidon, making his journey home so difficult. Although Tiresias told Odysseus he will make it home eventually, it will take a long time and he should remember to make homage to Poseidon on his return. He also cautioned Odysseus about touching the flocks of the sun on his journey home.

Odysseus spoke to his dead mother. She has died for loneliness of her son. He also viewed and talked to dead from Greek myths and the Trojan War. Agamemnon, who returned from the Trojan War only to be slain by his wife Clytemnestra, cautions Odysseus about his own wife, urging him to return to Ithaca in disguise and observe the situation discreetly.

Odysseus stops telling his tale at this point. He asks the Phaecians to let him sleep. His hosts, however, are eager to hear the rest of his tale, so he continues. He recounts how he tried to speak with Ajax, who killed himself after being disgraced by Odysseus, but Ajax refused to speak with him.

Some of the more mythical figures Odysseus saw are Heracles, the great warrior, Oedipus, who unknowingly married his own mother, the tortured souls Sisyphus and Tantalus, and the famed king Minos. The dead wanted to know about their loved ones in the mortal realm. Odysseus finally finds the experience overwhelming and made his escape back to the surface world.

BOOK 12: Odysseus and his men returned to Aeaea, home of Circes, and gave Elpenor a proper burial. Circe prepared Odysseus for his voyage by advising him on the Sirens, the Prowling Rocks, Scylla and Charybdis, and the island of Helios. Each of these places has its own unique danger.

The ship left, and their first challenge was the Sirens. These are beautiful women who sing and draw men to shipwreck on their coast. Odysseus commanded his crew to stuff their ears so they won't hear their song, but he himself wanted to hear it. He had himself tied to the mast so he couldn't escape, and when he heard their song he nearly went mad with longing. We might wonder why he didn't just plug up his ears like his sailors. Most likely it's because of his curiosity. Circe probably guessed that Odysseus would want to listen, but that there was great danger involved.

The next challenge was sailing between Charybdis (a violent whirlpool) and Scylla (a tentacled female monster with six heads). Six of Odysseus's men were devoured by Scylla as they pass between the two obstacles.

They next reached the island of Helios, Thrinacia. Odysseus had been cautioned (by both Tiresias and Circe) against touching the sun god's sheep there. The men obeyed, but they must stay there a month due to a storm. They ran out of food, and while Odysseus slept they ate some sheep. Helios was furious and asked Zeus to avenge his loss. The king of the gods hurtled lightning at Odysseus's ship, destroying it and killing all but

Odysseus. From there. Odysseus floated on wreckage from the ship for many days, finally arriving at Calypso's island. And from there he has already told his hosts the story, which he does not wish to repeat.

BOOK 13: The Phaecian people give Odysseus numerous gifts the next day. That evening, the ship sets sail for Ithaca. Odysseus sleeps heavily that night. When the ship arrives in Ithaca the next morning, they let him sleep and place his resting body on the island with his things.

The ship heads home. Poseidon realizes that Odysseus has finally made it home, enraging him. The god asks Zeus if he may avenge this injustice by hurting the Phaecian crew, and Zeus consents. Poseidon turns the ship to stone just as it is within reach of Scheria. The people of the island are horrified and vow to no longer help travelers.

Back on Ithaca, Odysseus wakes to find himself in a misty land. He thinks the Phaecians have deceived him and taken him to a strange island, not his home. He suspects they may have taken some of his treasure too, but this is not so. He comes across a young man and asks where he is, and learns it is indeed Ithaca. Rather than show delight and rush home, Odysseus pretends to be a foreigner. The lad reveals himself to be Athena in disguise, praising Odysseus for his cunning suspicion.

She tells Odysseus of the danger at his house. The suitors remain there, and Odysseus must use his mind to defeat them all. Disguising him as an old man, Athena tells Odysseus to go to his swineherd (the man who cares for his pigs) before going directly home. As for Athena, she will go to Telemachus (still abroad seeking news of Odysseus) and ensure his safe travel home.

BOOK 14: Odysseus arrives disguised at the home of

his swineherd, Eumaeus, who welcomes him. He has a small hut far from the house of Penelope and Telemachus. Eumaeus treats Odysseus like an honored guest, even though he has no reason to suspect his greatness. Even when Odysseus talks of fighting at Troy (not as Odysseus, but as another solider) and his wanderings after the war, Eumaeus is suspicious, but willing to indulge his guest. Odysseus tells Eumaeus that he has had word of Odysseus and that his master will arrive home soon. This apparent fabrication is too much for Eumaeus to tolerate and he tells Odysseus to stop.

They eat and Odysseus gathers further information on the men abusing his house, fueling his rage. When they sleep that night, Odysseus provides a further tale of the Trojan War and how Odysseus gave him his cloak when he was cold. Eumaeus is amused by the tale and provides his own cloak to the wandering stranger. Eumaeus's actions and words show Odysseus he is a faithful servant.

BOOK 15: Still at Menalaus's home in Sparta, Telemachus is visited by Athena and urged to go home, also advising caution in avoiding the suitors, who plot to kill Telemachus. He takes her warning seriously and wants to set out right away. His wakes his companion, Pisistratus (Nestor's son), who reminds Telemachus that without moonlight that night they won't be able to see. They wait till daylight to make their departure.

Menalaus wants to give them many gifts, but Telemachus tells him there is no time. What gifts they have are bestowed, and then an omen occurs. An eagle flies by carrying a goose. They are unclear what the sign means until Helen (Menalaus's wife) interprets it. She says it means Odysseus will soon be home to exact vengeance on the suitors in his home.

Telemachus and Pisistratus ride their chariot back to Pylos. In his urgency to leave, Telemachus asks Pisistratus to send his greeting to Nestor so he can make a speedy departure. Pisistratus agrees.

Before he boards his ship, Telemachus is approached by a man named Theoclymenus. This stranger begs Telemachus to provide him sanctuary. He is a man wanted for a murder he committed. Telemachus agrees to let the man board their ship.

Back in Ithaca, Odysseus is still with Eumaeus. Odysseus says he has overstayed his welcome and he must go to town to earn his keep. Perhaps he can work for the suitors of Penelope, he suggests. Eumaeus finds this suggestion distasteful and says Odysseus should stay with him. In a lengthy backstory, Eumaeus gives his own life story. Born the son of a king, he was kidnapped by pirates and then sold to Odysseus's father Laertes.

Telemachus and his ship arrive in Ithaca the next day. Theoclymenus is entrusted to a man in town named Piraeus, who agrees to shelter him.

Another omen is seen when a hawk flies by carrying a dove in its claws. This is again seen as favorable for Odysseus and his house.

BOOK 16: Telemachus comes to the hut of Eumaeus. He is greeted like a son by the old swineherd. Eumaeus introduces Odysseus and there is a brief recounting of Odysseus's fake history, with a suggestion that Odysseus stay at Telemachus's home. The young man cannot conceive of this while the suitors are at the house. He is afraid they will abuse the old man. Telemachus is still fearful for his own life, after all. Eumaeus is sent to Penelope to let her know Telemachus is home.

With Eumaeus gone, Athena urges Odysseus to reveal

himself as Telemachus's father. They have a tearful reunion and begin plotting the destruction of the suitors. Odysseus will enter his home as a beggar, risking abuse from the suitors, and Telemachus is not to interfere. Instead, his task is to remove the weapons of the suitors so they cannot access them when needed. There are a great many of them and Odysseus, although a great warrior, will need an advantage to overcome them.

Eumaeus tries to alert Penelope of Telemachus's homecoming discreetly, but a messenger from the ship soon tells the suitors that he is home. They are incensed that the young man has eluded them. Antinous proposes killing Telemachus outright before he has a chance to form an assembly and speak further against the suitors. Amphinomus, another suitor, urges caution and following the will of the gods. Penelope overhears their plotting and is disgusted. Another suitor, Eurymachus, smoothly lies and says they won't hurt her son.

BOOK 17: The next morning, Telemachus tells Eumaeus he is going to see his mother himself. Penelope has word of his arrival, but Telemachus knows her mind won't be at ease until she sees him. Telemachus goes to town and Eurycleia (a servant of Penelope) sees him first. Also at his family's home are Piraeus and Theoclymenus. Piraeus wants to bring Telemachus's treasures from his voyage to his home, but Telemachus is fearful of the suitors gaining possession of them.

Telemachus is met by his mother Penelope, and he tells her what news he gathered on his voyage. He doesn't yet tell her Odysseus is home. Theoclymenus exclaims that Odysseus is indeed on the island – he has no proof, but the omen of the birds has convinced him. Penelope is doubtful.

Odysseus heads to town now, accompanied by

Eumaeus. A man named Melanthius meets them on the way and abuses Odysseus (still disguised as a beggar). They get to Odysseus's home and are treated similarly by the suitors. Although the other suitors toss coins at the beggar, Antinous is particularly cruel and stingy, tossing a stool at Odysseus. Penelope takes pity on the beggar and asks him to come to her. Odysseus chooses to wait till later, however, so the suitors don't grow suspicious.

Eumaeus has to tend to the animals he cares for and must leave. He wishes Odysseus well and departs.

BOOK 18: A second beggar arrives at the house of Odysseus. He is called "Irus" and is a genuine beggar. He and Odysseus immediately irritate each other. A challenge is issued by Odysseus to fight the man. They fight and Irus is easily beaten by Odysseus. The suitors praise Odysseus for his fighting, especially Amphinomus, who gives Odysseus some food. In gratitude, Odysseus tries to warn Amphinomus away from the coming slaughter of the suitors. Athena keeps him there, however. He is destined to be killed by Telemachus, we're told.

Athena then prompts Penelope to make a rare appearance among the suitors (she usually avoids them). She is made especially beautiful by the goddess. Penelope goes down with the apparent notion of lecturing Telemachus on the recent fight allowed in her home. The suitors see her and Eurymachus praises her beauty. She speaks of the suitors in her home and says that Odysseus wished her to marry if he didn't return by the time Telemachus could grow a beard. That time has now passed, but she dislikes the suitors, who are more like parasites than anyone she'd marry. If they are suitors, where are their gifts for *her*? She asks them this and they decide to each bring her a gift. Odysseus finds this manipulation of the suitors by Penelope amusing.

Melantho, a housemaid, calls the beggar (Odysseus) a drunk and an old goat. He curses her back and scares her off.

Eurymachus then calls Odysseus lazy. Odysseus taunts him back and says he could beat Eurymachus in any fair contest. Angered, Eurymachus throws a stool at Odysseus, but misses and hits a servant.

Telemachus tells the men they are drunk and asks them to go to their beds. Amphinomus tells them he's right and the suitors go to sleep.

BOOK 19: With the suitors asleep, Telemachus and Odysseus remove the weapons from the hall. If the suitors should question them, Telemachus is to say he removes them to prevent an accident when they are drunk. Athena provides a magical light to let them see at night.

The housemaid Melantho sees Odysseus again and calls him a creepy old goat. He chastises her again and Penelope is also nearby to hear and speaks harshly to the maid. Penelope then has a bench brought so she and Odysseus may speak. He is hesitant to recount his painful history again, but offers a brief version of his story from Crete to the Trojan War to Ithaca. Penelope wants to hear of Odysseus. He gives her a detailed description that convinces her he tells the truth. He also shares the "rumors" he's heard of Odysseus's travels since the Trojan War. She tries to offer him a bed to sleep, but he resists as a beggar. She then suggests that a maid wash his feet. He refuses this too, unless an old maid can be found. There is one, Eurycleia, who nursed Odysseus as a child. As she cleans him she notices a scar on his leg from a hunting accident as a youth – the story of his injury by a boar is recounted. Eurycleia immediately knows that the old beggar is Odysseus. She wants to alert Penelope but Odysseus swears her to silence.

Penelope speaks again with Odysseus and recounts a dream she's had: Fat geese were feeding on the grain at the side of her house, when an eagle swooped down to break their necks. Odysseus interprets this as a vision of his own return to destroy the suitors. Penelope would like to believe this is so, but she fears the time has come to wed one of the suitors. She will provide a contest the next day. Each man will attempt to shoot an arrow through twelve ax heads (something Odysseus could do) and the winner will marry Penelope.

BOOK 20: Odysseus has trouble falling asleep. Housemaids go to have sex with the suitors and Odysseus is furious. He wonders if he should try to slaughter them all now, but remembers worse things he has endured (like the Cyclops). He expresses his doubts to Athena about the battle tomorrow and she reassures him the gods are on his side. Further omens appear and servants pray for Odysseus's return and vengeance.

In the early hours of the morning Eurycleia has the maids clean the house. She wants it to look its best for Odysseus's return. A goatherd named Melanthius comes in the hall and insults the beggar (Odysseus) allowed to sleep there. A more kindly man, Piloitios, an ox-herd, is more generous to Odysseus. This man curses the suitors and says he would move away were it not for loyalty to Odysseus.

The suitors consider killing Telemachus again, but decide to let him live for now. They feast instead. One of them named Ktesippos insults Odysseus and throws a cow's hoof shoe at the beggar. Odysseus dodges it but Telemachus is furious at the suitor. The men offer another token apology and say they'll do no more. Athena makes the suitors laugh hard, angering Telemachus and Odysseus further. The scene is building towards a climax when the family's rage will tolerate the suitors no more.

Theoclymenus, the young man Telemachus brought to Ithaca for sanctuary, visits the house and predicts a bad fate for the suitors. He sees blood in their future and darkness. Eurymachus mocks him and tries to send him out, but Theoclymenus leaves of his own accord. Once gone, the suitors mock Telemachus's choice in companions – a beggar and a madman making crazy predictions. Telemachus ignores them and waits for his father to begin the slaughter.

BOOK 21: Penelope gets the bow that Odysseus left behind when he left for the Trojan War. She cries at the memories it brings up of Odysseus. Explaining the shooting contest to the suitors, they are all eager to get an arrow through the twelve ax handles. Eumaeus the swineherd and Iphitos the Philoetius the cowherd are there, and they cry because it appears Odysseus won't return home in time. Odysseus follows them as they go outside, revealing himself as their master and asking them to aid him seal up the hall at the right time.

Before anyone can shoot an arrow, the bow must be bent and the string must be strung on it. Telemachus wants to try stringing it before the suitors, but he fails, or lets himself fail to give the suitors a chance to also fail. Some of the suitors then try the bow; none can string it. The suitors want to sacrifice to Apollo before they make any more attempts with bending the bow.

Then Odysseus speaks up. He wants a chance to bend it. The suitors are angry at the man's arrogance. Penelope insists they let the beggar try, but Telemachus tells her to mind her own business and leave this business to the men. Telemachus finally gives Odysseus permission to attempt bending it. Odysseus easily does it. Once strung there is a sound of thunder (Zeus) overhead. Odysseus aims and fires the bow through the twelve ax handles. Telemachus stands near his father and grabs his weapons for battle.

BOOK 22: Odysseus aims the bow at a second target, and shoots Antinous through the throat, killing him. The other suitors think it was a wild shot. They don't realize that Odysseus intends to kill them all. The beggar tells them he is Odysseus. The suitors say they will pay him back for the food used at his house. Odysseus refuses. Eurymachus calls the suitors to fight Odysseus, but he begins killing them with arrows. Telemachus helps his father, killing Amphinomus with a spear (as foreshadowed earlier). Telemachus then runs to get more equipment for Odysseus, himself, Eumaeus and Philoetius.

Melanthius the goatherd offers to help the suitors. He will climb the wall to a storage chamber where he knows the suitors' weapons have been put away. He gets the equipment as planned and Telemachus blames himself for leaving the storeroom door open. Eumaeus and Philoetius go to investigate. They capture the treacherous Melanthius and tie him to the roof for now.

Odysseus's friend Mentor appears (once again, this is Athena in disguise). He encourages Odysseus in the face of overwhelming odds. Odysseus is rallied, and the slaughter continues. Ktesippos, who had thrown the cow hoof at Odysseus, faces a gruesome death. The sign of Athena, a great shield, appears in the hall, frightening the suitors further. They know they are doomed.

Leodes, a fortuneteller for the suitors, begs to be

spared. Odysseus kills him. Phemios the minstrel also begs for his life, and with Telemachus's word, he is spared. Also spared is the herald Medon.

When all the suitors are dead, Odysseus calls for Eurycleia and has her fetch the maidservants unfaithful to his authority. He has them clean the hall of suitors and their blood, and then he takes the women outside to hang them.

Melanthius is brought down from the roof, his genitals removed and fed to the dogs, and then he is hacked to pieces.

When the killing is done, Odysseus calls his household to show them all that he is returned. They purify the hall with fire. The only one unaware of Odysseus's return is Penelope, and she has been kept in a mystical sleep by the gods.

BOOK 23: Eurycleia wakes Penelope and tells her that the beggar is Odysseus and that he's slain the suitors. Penelope first thinks the old nurse is mocking her, and then that Eurycleia has been deceived by the gods.

Penelope goes to Odysseus and Telemachus reprimands her for remaining distant from her husband. Odysseus is unperturbed and says they must plan for the reaction from the townspeople. They have slain some of the best men in the land and that will not bode well with their families. Odysseus and Telemachus will travel away from town for a while. As they prepare, the minstrel strikes up some music so anyone passing will think Penelope has finally married a suitor.

To test Odysseus, Penelope says that his bed will be moved outside his bedchamber for him to sleep on. Odysseus is furious because he knows the bed cannot be moved, that he constructed it himself from a tree trunk that he carved away, and that he built the entire bedroom around it. Penelope sees by his knowledge that he really is Odysseus and she finally goes to him as his wife.

Odysseus explains that he cannot stay long in the house. He promised Tiresias he would make a voyage on the coast until a sign was given, and there make a sacrifice to Poseidon. He also tells her of his long voyage home from Troy.

That night, Odysseus and Penelope make love and he sleeps there. The next day, Odysseus heads off to do the things he must, first going to the orchard of his father Laertes. He commands Penelope to stay in her room and see no one but her servants while he is gone.

BOOK 24: The scene shifts to Hades, where Hermes has led the souls of the dead suitors. They meet some of the heroes of the Trojan War, who want to know how so many strong young men suddenly find themselves dead. The suitors explain how Odysseus vanquished them all, and they refuse to accept responsibility for their deaths. Agamemnon laughs and praises Penelope as an honest woman, unlike his own wife Clytemnestra, who plotted his murder.

Back in Ithaca, Odysseus goes to his father's country home. He finds Laertes (his father) tending his garden. Odysseus doesn't immediately reveal his identity, first spinning one of his many stories, but soon relenting and telling his father the truth. Laertes asks for proof and Odysseus shows his scar and tells him details to prove himself. Odysseus explains his fear that the families of the dead suitors will come after him seeking vengeance.

The scene shifts to a meeting of these very families. Many are angry for blood. Antinous's father is particularly mad. A group of these relatives march to

Laertes's home and a battle starts. Athena intervenes in the form of Mentor, and with Zeus's aid the bloodshed is ended, the need for vengeance vanishing from all.

CRITICAL QUESTIONS & ESSAY TOPICS

These critical questions may be answered in a variety of ways based on your reading of the text. I have provided suggestions in the answers below, and I encourage you to consider alternative answers as you explore these topics.

1. What keeps Odysseus away from home for so long?

The war keeps Odysseus away for ten years, but an additional ten years elapse before he gets home to Ithaca. The cause of his delay can be traced to Poseidon, whom Odysseus angered by blinding his son Polyphemous. But the story makes it clear that Odysseus might have escaped the curse of the Cyclops if he hadn't voiced his identity. Odysseus, like every great hero, has his weaknesses. Pride and curiosity are his most notable faults, but they also make him great as well. Without these, there would be no story.

2. What is the role of family in *The Odyssey*?

The bond of family is one of the strongest

connections in the story. People are expected to honor their families and maintain harmonious relationships with them. We see this in Telemachus and Penelope staying loyal to Odysseus, but also to Poseidon avenging his son Polyphemous, Pisistratus helping Nestor at his father's instruction, and numerous other examples. The few times when family bonds are ignored (for example, Clytemnestra plotting Agamemnon's murder), the violators are heavily condemned and criticized.

3. How are women portrayed in the story?

Women play key roles throughout the story. Athena, the goddess of battle, is a strong figure that often protects Odysseus. Penelope uses her wits to hold off the suitors. Nausicaa and Arete do their part to sway Alcinous and help Odysseus. Eurycleia is instrumental and protecting Odysseus from the suitors.

Despite their many strengths, there is also a double standard toward female sexuality in the book. Women are usually blamed for affairs, not men, and Odysseus's flings with Circe and Calypso are viewed as necessary to the "adventurous life." The sexual favors that the maidservants give the suitors is particularly frowned upon by men and women alike.

4. What is the relationship between humanity and the gods in *The Odyssey*?

Athena has the strongest ties with Odysseus in the book. She always keeps an eye on him to ensure his survival. Zeus is less interested in the affairs of men, mainly intervening when Athena or Poseidon petitions him to do so. The gods generally treat humanity as its playthings and little more.

5. How do vengeance and honor shape the narrative and conflict?

An enormous amount of *The Odyssey*'s actions are determined by honor and vengeance. The society has extremely strong expectations about individual behavior. Those who fail to meet these standards are punished as outcasts, rebels, or demented souls.

Vengeance comes into play throughout the text. The Trojan War was launched to avenge the wrong done by Paris to Menalaus. Poseidon's vengeance is what keeps Odysseus from home for ten years after the war. And Odysseus's vengeance against the suitors is the climax of the book. The only thing that stops the cycle of vengeance (in the last chapter) is the intervention of the gods. Vengeance is firmly linked to honor in ancient Greece. A violation of honor obligates one to seek vengeance.

6. How does Odysseus develop as a character?

Although Odysseus doesn't change as much as Telemachus, for instance, he does develop. One of his great weaknesses is pride, and this is what nearly kills him after escaping from Polyphemous. But by the time he arrives home he has learned enough caution and subtlety to abstain from directly challenging the suitors. If he allowed his pride to take control he never would have been able to act as a beggar and take the abuse of the men in his home. He has clearly develops patience, caution, and humility in the book.

CONCLUSION

The Odyssey is a classic story, as exciting today as when it was first released. Its characters remain beloved in modern literature, and its ideas are still being absorbed by each generation that reads it. I hope this guide has helped you navigate this book, and deepened your understanding of all that occurs in its pages.

Made in the USA
Middletown, DE
23 October 2015